NOW YOU CAN READ....
JOHN THE BAPTIST

STORY RETOLD BY ARLENE C. ROURKE

ILLUSTRATED BY GWEN GREEN

Published by Rourke Publications, Inc., P.O. Box 3328, Vero Beach, Florida 32964. Copyright © 1985 by Rourke Publications, Inc. All copyrights reserved. No part of this book may be reproduced in any form without written permission from the publisher. Printed in the United States of America.

The Publishers acknowledge permission from Brimax Books for the use of the name "Now You Can Read" and "Large Type For First Readers" which identify Brimax Now You Can Read series.

Library of Congress Cataloging in Publication Data

Rourke, Arlene, 1944-
    John the Baptist.

    Summary: Briefly retells the life of John, cousin of Jesus, who prophesied the coming of the Son of God and baptized many people.
    1. John, the Baptist, Saint—Juvenile literature.
2. Bible. N.T.—Biography—Juvenile literature.
3. Christian saints—Palestine—Biography—Juvenile literature. [1. John, the Baptist, Saint. 2. Bible stories—N.T.]   I. Title.
BS2456.R67 1985   232.9'4 [B]   85-19678
ISBN 0-86625-317-3

GROLIER ENTERPRISES CORP.

NOW YOU CAN READ. . . .
JOHN THE BAPTIST

As you know, Baby Jesus was born
in Bethlehem many years ago. He
was born to a girl named Mary. Did
you know that Mary had a cousin
named Elizabeth? This is the story
of Elizabeth and her husband,
Zachariah. But, most of all, it is the
story of their son, John.

Elizabeth and Zachariah were good people. They had been married for many years and loved each other very much. They had only one sadness. They had never had a child. Now they were very old and they thought it was too late for Elizabeth to have a baby.

One day, an angel
appeared to Zachariah.
"Do not be afraid," said the angel.
"I am Gabriel and I bring good news.
You and Elizabeth will have a son.
You will call him John. He will be a
great man, filled with the spirit of
God. He will prepare the way for the
saviour, Jesus Christ."

Zachariah was amazed. "This cannot be true," he said "My wife and I are too old to have a child." "I am Gabriel, the messenger of God," spoke the angel. "I speak the truth. Because you do not believe me, you will be struck dumb. You will not be able to speak until what I have said comes true." Zachariah hurried home.

He wrote down all that had happened to him. He gave the words to Elizabeth. She was thrilled! At last, she could have the child she longed for.

When John was born, there was
much happiness. Everyone came to
see the new baby and bring gifts.
As the angel had promised, Zachariah
was able to speak again.

John and his parents lived on the edge of the desert. As a boy, he spent much of his time alone. He would go off by himself to think.

He felt that God had chosen him for a special mission. As he grew, this feeling became stronger and stronger.

When John became a man, he went
into the wilderness to live alone.
The wilderness
was a barren land
between Jerusalem
and the Dead Sea.
He spent all his time
thinking about God.

He was tall and thin and wore simple,
rough clothing. He ate whatever grew
wild.

At last, John knew it was time to tell people about the coming of Jesus. He came out of the wilderness and lived on the banks of the Jordan River. The Jordan was a big river and many people passed by it.

John preached to the people and told
them that the Son of God would soon
be among them. Many people
listened to John. He baptized them
in the waters of the river. He became
known as John the Baptist.

One day, a young man appeared in
the crowd.
"Behold the Lamb of God," John
said, seeing Jesus.

"I wish to be baptized," said Jesus.
John was amazed. He did not think
that the Son of God would want to be
baptized by him.
"Do as I say," Jesus went on. "Only
in this way will God's will be done."

And so, John baptized Jesus in the Jordan River. The spirit of God came down in the shape of a dove. A voice came out of the clouds and said, "This is my beloved Son in whom I am well pleased."

Afterward, Jesus and John went their separate ways. Each of them preaching about God. Jesus had now begun His public life.

In those days, there lived a king named Herod. Herod had done a wicked thing. He had married his brother's wife. Many people did not like what Herod had done. Because he was the king they were afraid to speak against him.

John was not afraid of Herod. He told the people that Herod should give up his sinful life. Herod did not like what John had said about him. Herod's wife did not like it either.

One day, John was preaching to a crowd of people. A group of soldiers rode up.

Quickly, they walked up to John.

"Are you John the Baptist?" asked the captain.

"Yes, I am," answered John.

"You must come with us," said the captain. "King Herod has ordered your arrest."

John was put into prison. At last, Herod felt safe. Now John could not talk against him. Herod's wife was not as sure.

One night, King Herod and his wife held a great feast. Many people came. There was lots to eat and drink. Everyone was having a good time. A girl named Salome danced for them. She was the daughter of Herod's wife. Her dance pleased Herod so much that he offered to grant her any wish. Her mother had told her what to ask for.

"I want John the Baptist killed," she said. Herod had no choice but to give her what she asked.

Many people wept when they heard of John's death. But, John was happy with God. He had done what God wanted him to do.

All these appear in the pages of the story. Can you find them?

Zachariah

The Captain

Elizabeth

Salome

Herod's wife

John the Baptist

Now tell the story in your own words.

Step-by-Step Transformations
Turning Wax into Crayons

Herald McKinley

Cavendish
Square
New York

Published in 2015 by Cavendish Square Publishing, LLC
243 5th Avenue, Suite 136, New York, NY 10016

Website: cavendishsq.com

This publication represents the opinions and views of the author based on his or her personal experience, knowledge, and research. The information in this book serves as a general guide only. The author and publisher have used their best efforts in preparing this book and disclaim liability rising directly or indirectly from the use and application of this book.

CPSIA Compliance Information: Batch #WS14CSQ

All websites were available and accurate when this book was sent to press.

Library of Congress Cataloging-in-Publication Data
McKinley, Herald.
Turning wax into crayons / Herald McKinley.
pages cm. — (Step-by-step transformations)
Includes index.
ISBN 978-1-62712-366-2 (hardcover) ISBN 978-1-62712-490-4 (paperback) ISBN 978-1-62713-003-5 (ebook)
1. Crayons—Juvenile literature. 2. Manufacturing processes—Juvenile literature. I. Title.

NC870.M38 2014
741.2'3—dc23

2014001538

Editorial Director: Dean Miller
Editor: Amy Hayes
Copy Editor: Cynthia Roby
Art Director: Jeffrey Talbot
Designer: Joseph Macri
Photo Researcher: J8 Media
Production Manager: Jennifer Ryder-Talbot
Production Editor: David McNamara

The photographs in this book are used by permission and through the courtesy of: Cover photos by AP Photo/Steve Klaver; Tim Perdue/ Flickr Open/Getty Images; © iStockphoto.com/pkdirector, 5; ©The Star-Ledger/Frank Conlon/The Image Works, 7; Photos courtesy Crayola, used with permission. ©2015 Crayola LLC. Crayola® and Serpentine Design® are trademarks of Crayola, 9, 11, 15, 19; William Thomas Cain/Getty Images, 13; AP Photo/Rick Smith, 17; /Blend Images/SuperStock, 21; Back Cover: Derek E. Rothchild/The Image Bank/Getty Images.

Printed in the United States of America

Contents

Crayons are made from **wax**.

5

First, the wax is heated.

Wax **melts** when it is hot.

Colored **powder** is mixed
into the hot wax.

The wax becomes the same
color as the powder.

Next, the colored wax is poured into a **mold**.

The mold will form the wax into the shape of crayons.

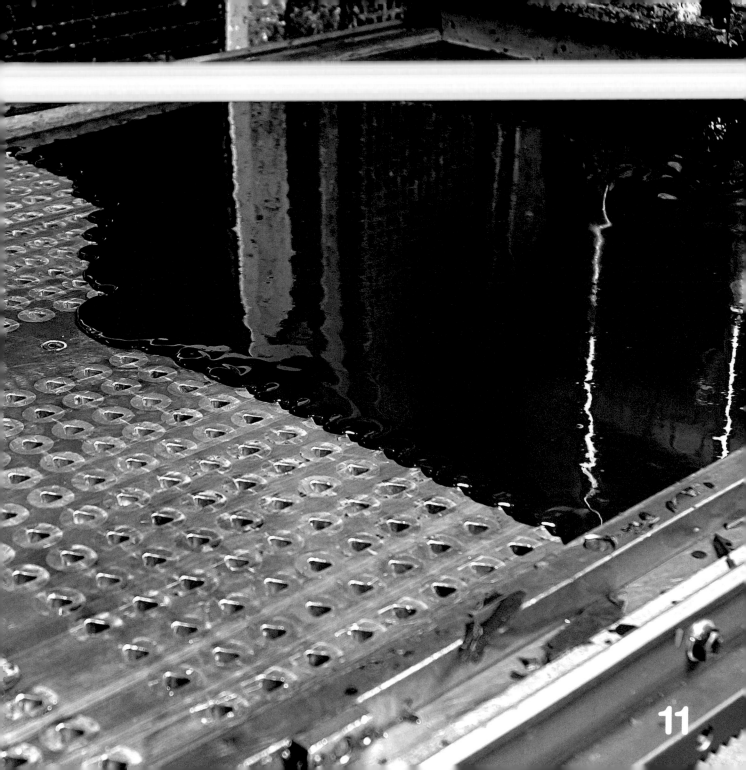

11

As the wax cools, it becomes hard.

The hard wax is taken out of the mold.

The wax is now in the shape of crayons.

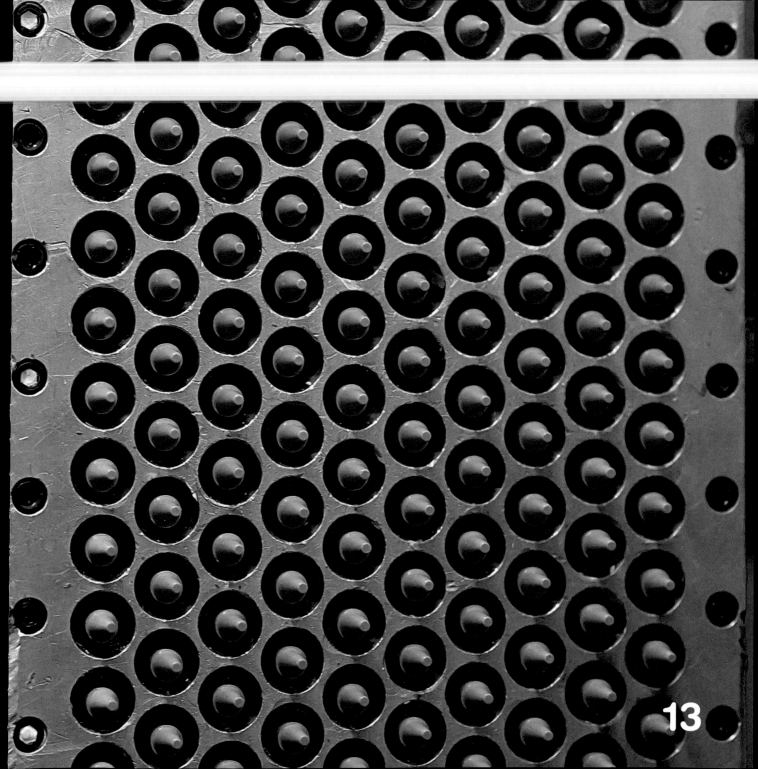

13

A worker looks at the crayons.

He makes sure the crayons are not broken.

15

Then, a machine puts **labels** on each crayon.

17

The finished crayons are put
into boxes.

Now, the crayons are ready
to be used.

We use crayons to draw and color on paper.

Crayons are fun to use.

Words to Know

crayons (KRAY-unz) – colored wax sticks used for drawing or coloring

labels (LAY-buhlz) – pieces of paper that are attached to something and give information

melts (MELTS) – when heat makes something change from being solid to being liquid

mold (MOHLD) – a hollow container that you can pour liquid into so that it sets in that shape

powder (POW-dur) – tiny particles of a solid substance

wax (WAKS) – a substance made from fats and oils

Find Out More

Books

How is a Crayon Made?

Oz Charles

Scholastic

What Happens at a Crayon Factory?

Lisa M. Guidone

Gareth Stevens

Website

PBS Kids

Mister Rogers' Neighborhood

pbskids.org/rogers/video_crayons.html

Index